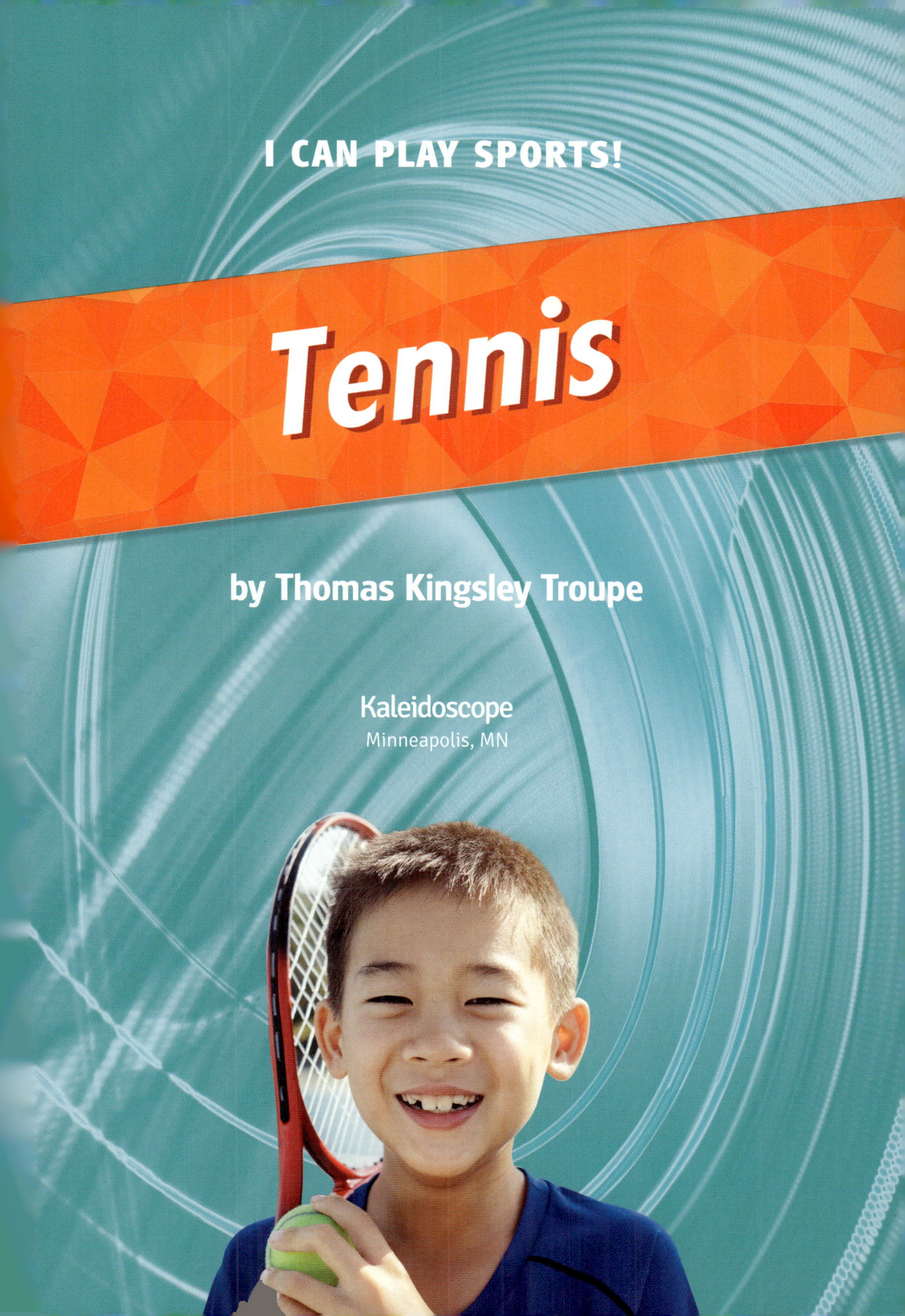

I CAN PLAY SPORTS!

Tennis

by Thomas Kingsley Troupe

Kaleidoscope
Minneapolis, MN

Where the Quest for Discovery Begins

This edition first published in 2023 by Kaleidoscope Publishing, Inc.

Kaleidoscope Publishing, Inc.
6012 Blue Circle Drive
Minnetonka, MN 55343

Library of Congress Control Number
2022937562

ISBN
978-1-64519-589-4 (library bound)
978-1-64519-659-4 (ebook)

Bigfoot Jr. lurks within one of the images in this book. It's up to you to find him!

Table of Contents

To the Net

The tennis player tosses the ball up. The **racquet** smashes it across the net.

The ball flies over the net. It bounces once. The player runs to the ball. The **serve** is returned. I can play tennis!

Tennis is a sport played with two or four players. It is played on a tennis **court**.

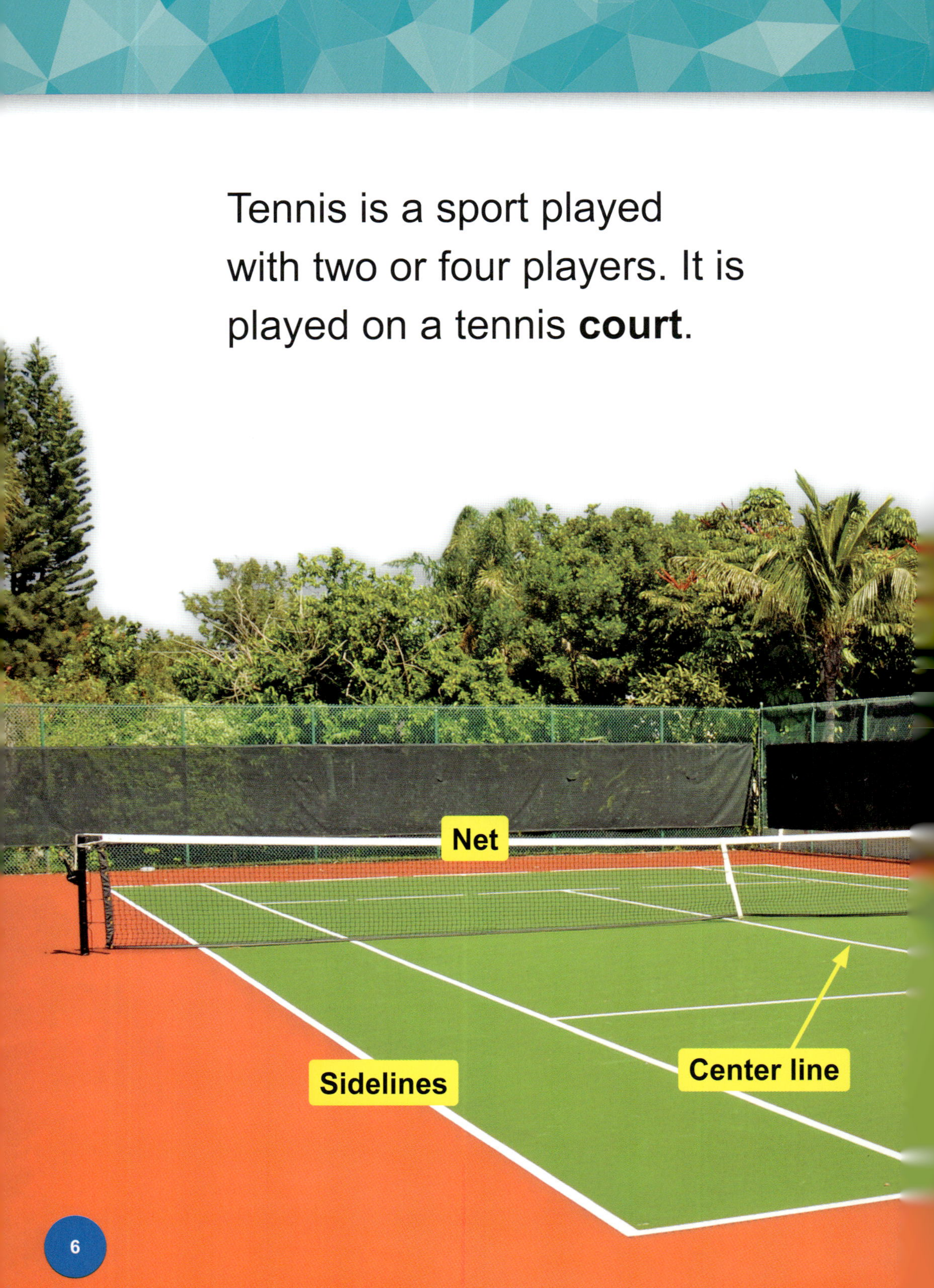

The courts can be indoors or outside. Courts are made of grass, concrete, or clay.

A tennis court has a net in the middle. The ball is hit over the net each time.

There are lines around a tennis court. The ball needs to stay inside these **sidelines** and baselines.

FUN FACT

The sport of tennis was invented in 1873 in England.

Meet the Player

Tennis players use racquets to hit the ball. They wear shorts or skirts and tennis shoes.

Some players wear **sweatbands** on their heads or wrists. It keeps the sweat out of their eyes.

Tennis players learn many different **strokes**. Each type of stroke is for a different purpose.

Some strokes hit the ball far. Other strokes smash the ball fast or knock it over the net.

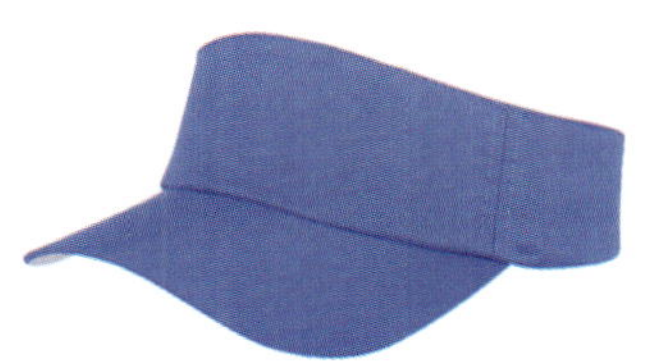

FUN FACT

Venus Williams has won the most Olympic medals in tennis. She has 4 gold medals and 1 silver.

Overhead Smash

Each round of tennis is called a match. Each match is made up of four points.

To start, a player hits the ball over the net. This first hit is called a serve.

FUN FACT

Most tennis balls were white until 1972. Yellow tennis balls are easier to see on television.

There are five basic skills in tennis

1 Footwork
being able to run to the ball on the court

2 Serving
hitting the ball over the net to start the point

3 Forehand
being able to return the ball with the player's forearm facing the net

4 Backhand
being able to return the ball with the player's back of the hand facing the net

5 Volleying
keeping the ball going back and forth across the net

Hitting the ball back and forth is called a **volley**.

The ball can only bounce once before it is hit again.

Game Point

Tennis players are trying to score points. When their **opponent** misses a ball, they get a point.

They don't want to hit the ball into the net or outside the court. The other player will score.

FUN FACT

Sam Groth made the fastest tennis serve ever. The ball went 163.7 mph (263.4 km/h)!

When a player scores four points, they win the game. But, then the players usually play more! If they win six games, they win a set.

If a player wins two or three sets, they win the match. Let's play tennis again!

Photo Glossary

court: The area with a net where tennis is played.

opponent: The player on the other side of the net.

racquet: The object used to hit the ball in a game of tennis.

serve: When a player hits the ball to begin a point.

sidelines: The lines around a tennis court.

strokes: The types of strikes used to hit the tennis ball.

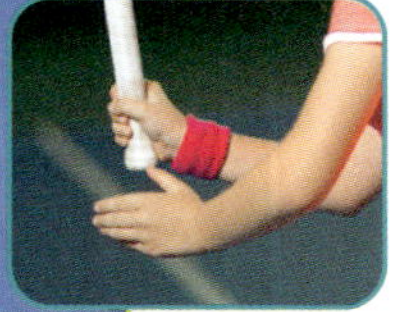

sweatbands: The fabric worn around the player's head or wrists to block sweat.

volley: When players keep the ball in the air before it hits the court.

Read More

Bussiere, Desiree. *Tennis By the Numbers.* Mankato, MN, ABDO Publishing, 2013.

Derr, Aaron. *Tennis: An Introduction to Being a Good Sport.* Minneapolis, MN, Lerner Publishing, 2017.

Poray Goddu, Krystyna. *Serena Williams.* Mankato, MN, Black Rabbit Books, 2020.

Websites

FACTSURFER

Factsurfer.com gives you a safe, fun way to find more information.

1. Go to www.factsurfer.com.
2. Enter "Tennis" into the search box and click 🔍
3. Select your book cover to see a list of related websites.

About the Author

Thomas Kingsley Troupe has been reading and writing stories from a very young age. He's the author of over 100 books for kids of all ages. When he's not putting words together, he's fixing his house, watching movies, ghost-hunting or thinking about taking a nap. Thomas lives in Woodbury, MN, with his two ridiculous sons.

INDEX

PHOTO CREDITS

The images in this book are reproduced through the courtesy of: Cool_photo/Shutterstock Images, cover (top/girl); azure1/Shutterstock Images, cover (ball); SewCream/Shutterstock Images, cover, 1 (boy); Veronica Louro/Shutterstock Images, p. 3; pajtica/Shutterstock Images, p. 4–5, 22 (serve); FamVeld/Shutterstock Images, p. 5; Mark Winfrey/Shutterstock Images, p. 6–7, 22 (court); Kaspars Grinvalds/Shutterstock Images, p. 8; Steve Collender/Shutterstock Images, p. 9, 22 (sidelines); zydesign/Shutterstock Images, p. 9 (Fun Fact); Max kegfire/Shutterstock Images, p. 10; Happy Stock Photo/Shutterstock Images, p. 11 (sweatbands); domnitsky/Shutterstock Images, p. 11 (headband); Master1305/Shutterstock Images, p. 11; Elkhophoto/Shutterstock Images, p. 12; SVRSLYIMAGE/Shutterstock Images, p. 13 (top); Jair Ferreira Belafacce/Shutterstock Images, p. 13 (visor); action sports/Shutterstock Images, p. 13 (Fun Fact); Cool_photo/Shutterstock Images, p. 14; Dmytro Flisak/Shutterstock Images, p. 15 (ball); O.PASH/Shutterstock Images, p. 15 (net); photokup/Shutterstock Images, p. 15 (Fun Fact); Elkhophoto/Shutterstock Images, p. 16 (footwork); Master1305/Shutterstock Images, p. 16 (serving); Akaberka/Shutterstock Images, p. 16, 22 (forehand, strokes); Elkhophoto/Shutterstock Images, p. 16 (backhand); makieni/Shutterstock Images, p. 16 (volleying); Olena Yakobchuk/Shutterstock Images, p. 17 (volley); Elkhophoto/Shutterstock Images, p. 18; Julio Yeste/Shutterstock Images, p. 20; Pressmaster/Shutterstock Images, p. 21, 22 (opponent); Patrick Foto/Shutterstock Images, p. 21 (bottom); pukach/Shutterstock Images, p. 22 (racquet); Cool_photo/Shutterstock Images, p. 22 (sweatbands); azure1/Shutterstock Images, p. 23.